COMET
Goes to the Farm

by Nancy Ronan
and
🐾 COMET

Copyright © 2021 Nancy Ronan
All rights reserved.
ISBN: 978-1-7359255-9-2

My name is Comet.
I am a Golden Retriever.

One of my favorite things to do is to visit the farm!

I've been going to the farm since I was a puppy.

This is my sister Clementine.
She likes to go to the farm too.

There are all kinds of animals at the farm.

Some of them are babies, like this chick.

The baby chicks will grow into big chickens.

Some animals have jobs.
The barn cats catch mice.

My cat's job is to snuggle with me!

I visit goats like Billy with his small pointy ears

and Clover with floppy ears just like mine!

Clementine likes to sniff the little pink piglets.

The piglets like to sniff her too.

The donkeys, Rosie and Daisy, wear blankets in the winter

and fly masks in the summer.

Peanut is a miniature horse.
He is just my size.

Murray isn't my size, but he is my color.

I love my horse friends, big and small.

I even got to ride one when I was a puppy!

These are alpacas. They are fluffy and have big eyes.

I don't get too close because sometimes they spit.

The baby cow says moo when we stop to say hello.

The big cows do too.

My favorite thing to do at the farm is to roll in poop!

My least favorite thing is getting a bath afterwards.

After my bath, I dream about my next adventure.

There are so many places to see and sniff.

See you next time for some more fun!

Made in the USA
Middletown, DE
20 November 2021